ISHVARA

The realization of the Self with

the 29 cards of Ishvara

Paintings of Maria Theresia Bitterli

The texts have been translated

by Alex Dawson.

Studio ISHVARA

Studioishvara © 2019

ISBN 9783750402591

Herstellung und Verlag:
BoD - Books on Demand,
Norderstedt

www.studioishvara.com

SOMMARIO

INTRODUCTION

In the Vedic texts, Ishvara is described as the highest personification of the divine that can be imagined through the mind. Ishvara is like the wind, you don't see her/him but you hear her/him. The multitude is his/her manifestation. S/he also manifests him/herself through us. S/he is just a signpost that shows the way to ourselves, towards our Essence. Ishvara is our mirror of the soul. Ishvara is for those who are ready to go beyond both form and non-form.

We begin a journey of self-knowledge with Ishvara's oracle. This is a journey that begins with the call of the soul, that voice that from the depths of our dreams whispers to go in search of the inner, spiritual wealth and beauty of our life in the realization of the Self.

1. WHO WE ARE

Be what you are, because you cannot be otherwise. You are already what you are looking for. You are beyond the memory of the past, beyond time and space. Learn to know yourselves better and you will understand that even if you are different from each other, you all come from the same source. You are what witnesses the coming and the going of the breath, and of Consciousness itself. Always see yourselves as God's instruments.

2. VALID HUMAN RELATIONS

Sometimes, some expressed human aspects are difficult to understand and even more to accept. First, learn to take time to stay at peace with yourselves, alone, and you will discover that, observing your mental patterns and becoming increasingly aware, they will lose strength and hold of you. Only then you will be able to meet the other in the here and now without the influence of the past. And valid human relationships can always be new and creative. Deep relationships create human values based on mutual respect and mutual understanding.

3. PAIN, SUFFERING

Don't think of escaping pain. Learn more and more to enter the pain and surrender to it. You will completely transcend pain when you realize that you are Eternity. Too much focus on the body distracts you from Eternity. Why worry so much about what sooner of later you'll have to give up (the body)? Mystics and saints of every religion have shown that it is possible to experience mystical ecstasy, even if their body and mind had pain and suffering.

4. TIME

Reaction is always from the past. Thought is the past which, changing itself in the present, projects itself into the future. Your nostalgia for the past blurs your ability to perceive the eternal new beauty of the present moment. Human times are very long, spiritual ones are immediate. Divine grace is beyond time and space. It will decide how and when the Self will be realized.

5. HIERARCHY AND DIVERSITY

The hierarchy, in essence, is one, in manifestation it is expressed in diversity. The Sun, for example, can be seen as the highest hierarchy for you, because without it there would be no life, but it does not command you, or tells you what to do. The Sun shines on everyone, it does not distinguish between good and bad. Each of you is a master and a disciple, and a pure transcendence of both.

6. THE DREAM

The magic of the present moment, in the here and now, opens your hearts. Learn more and more to relax in the here and now, regardless of what you are doing. Everything you need to fulfill your dream will come to you in due course, so relax more and more.

Live your life as if it were a magnificent dream full of beauty, because all states of consciousness, including the waking state, are of the consistency of a dream in the eyes of the Self, because they are fleeting. So, decide now, in this moment, to be happy. Thus, life becomes a blessing, an unmissable opportunity for growth in joy and in Love.

7. MIRROR AND PROJECTION

Even if your life has its own daily rhythm, always listen to your heart, which, within the limits of your possibilities, helps you to discern what is best for you. Remember that, whether you remain still or run, peace always reigns within you, therefore, observe it, in the here and now, and you will discover that it has always been here, within you, and always will be, even when this body-mind will stop working, this extraordinary inner peace will continue to exist, and this is eternity. You are eternity, your body and your mind are made of eternity. Body and mind are born and reabsorbed by eternity, which is infinite peace, within you, here and now. Your mind is the screen, the mirror in which what you see appears, what you experience in your life. The more you identify with the mind, with the image you have of yourself, the more you will suffer its dissolution. If, on the other hand, you recognize yourself in the inner silence that precedes the mind, then there will no longer be anyone who can identify with the mirror and suffer, since you will observe life from the perspective of this immeasurable silence. You are this infinite silence, which is space without boundaries, a void where neither time nor space exist, but only pure love, pure awareness, which manifests itself in this moment, here and now, and which is made of the same essence, therefore, every form of separation is transcended. From this silence, you witness and observe what happens in your consciousness. You observe what you are, what happens to your body-mind. You no longer identify with what is projected onto the screen of your consciousness. You precede what you think you are. Inner silence is the Self, which unites and transcends every thing, there is no more separation.

8. DESTINY

Destiny is absolved in any case, therefore, abandon yourselves totally to it, not as a depressing form of resigned nihilism but, on the contrary, with full awareness of happily fulfilling what was established by the divine plan. Always remember that your wills and responsibilities are part of the divine plan. You are the world and the world are you. The destiny that you are living now is your compass and, living every act in the here and now towards total freedom, will lead you to the awakening of pure love. Chance admits ignorance, but freedom transcends both.

9. THE TEACHER

Spiritual teachers are there to remind you of what you have forgotten. You have forgotten what you cannot remember. Not all Masters can lead you to the Self, some give you techniques that limit you. Free yourself from the image you have of the Master, otherwise you will continue to be in a cage. A true Master frees you, does not put you in a cage. What need is there to worship an image when you know you are the Absolute? Nevertheless, nothing prevents you from venerating an image, knowing that you are the Absolute.

10. BEYOND DUALITY AND NON-DUALITY

Duality should be transcended with meditation. Your dual mind will never accept the fact that you are eternal. Once unity is achieved, there is no turning back. It is basically a fusion between the I and the Self. The deception of your mind is to make you mistakenly believe that you are separated from the world, but even if you are different, you are not separated. In fact, you cannot be because you are the fruit of the world, and as such, you cannot be separated from it. You are the world. If there is no separation, then there is totality, and you will live your life fully. The wave is not separated from the ocean. Duality and non-duality are the two sides of the same coin. Meditation unites them and transcends them.

11. PARALLEL WORLDS OF THE MULTIVERSE

There are infinite parallel worlds that can be described in as many infinite ways. Meditation is not an escape to other worlds, on the contrary, it always flourishes in the here and now, bringing its fruits into everyday life.

12. IMPERMANENCE

Birth and death are illusory because they are impermanent. Paying too much attention to impermanence takes you away from the Self. By incarnating you have lost the eternal dimension and, to find it again, you should rediscover what you were before you were conceived. Eternity is beyond impermanence and permanence. In non-separation everything is Eternity. Pure awareness is the Eternity that witnesses the coming and going of the different states of consciousness.

13. MEDITATION

You should take more time to meditate, because all the answers to your questions are already within you. By meditating, you will increasingly realize that you are not all what you believe to be. If you are aware of who is meditating, it does not matter what the object of meditation is. Start meditating by being aware of what you are in the here and now. Meditate on the form and later on the non-form and the inner silence will be your Master.

14. THE MANTRA OM NAMÒ ISHVARAYA NAMAHA

This mantra is a fusion of very ancient mantras and is a praise to the Absolute. Each mantra benefits from the divinity to which it is addressed. This mantra is recommended for those who are hungry but are not satisfied with recipes. It is the mantra that will be revealed to you without you having to repeat it voluntarily. Let it dance with joy in your mind. Don't have rules, let the mantra recite itself. Don't force anything. Let its reciting happen spontaneously. Do not block or brake when the mantra is born out of the silence of your mind. Do not become too technical otherwise you will lose the deep meaning of the mantra. The mantra leads you to God. The mantra is the highest form of prayer. Both are born and dissolve in the silence of the mind.

15. LIFE IS HERE AND NOW

One should not seek suffering but the joy of living. No sacrifice is required to reach God, unless foreseen by the divine plan. It is not necessary that you sacrifice yourself, after all who are you, if not nothingness, emptiness, silence, everything!? We should abandon ourselves totally to life in order to be born again in every moment. Enjoy every moment of life without regrets or attachments. Never exclude anything from life because everything is always possible. Life is a continuous renewal. Learn to see the extraordinary in the ordinary. There is only what is, the here and now. Make every moment of your life a celebration of the sacred.

16. FREE WILL

Free will is not overridden by God or any teacher. Free will exists as long as you consider yourself a body-mind only. Always decide as if you have free will, this will help you feel more responsible and responsibility opens

the doors of compassion, which is
Love.

17. THE SILENT MIND

The mind can only lie to you because it is always limited. Doubts are of the mind. The mind lies; therefore, you listen to others instead of trusting yourself. Once all concepts have been abandoned, the mind enters into a profound and ecstatic silence, at which point you will have transcended all forms of individuality and separation, and the mind will be sacred in the realization of the Self, sinking into Eternity. Be increasingly aware of the depth of silence that is in your mind. Silence is the highest form of wisdom. A silent mind knows how to listen and accept the beauty of life because it is extraordinarily sensitive. Form and non-form embrace each other in the depth of a silent mind.

18. THE DIVINE PLAN

The mind, being limited, will never be able to fully understand why we abandon ourselves to the divine will. You can fight whole lives, but only if it is in the divine plan will you realize what you want. Nothing is wrong, everything is divine plan. No sacrifice is required to achieve what you want, unless foreseen for by the divine plan. When you realize that the mind can never completely know the divine plan, you relax, you abandon yourself more and more to the divine will, then your mind becomes more and more silent and, from this profound silence, the right action springs, which is in tune with the divine plan, and this is the flowering of love and compassion.

19. FREEDOM

Freedom is not doing what you want and like, this is childishness, immaturity and irresponsibility. Free yourself from all psychological conditioning by watching your thoughts influence your mind throughout the day. The knowledge of yourself that comes from observing what you actually are from moment to moment frees you from any conditioning, from any conflict, bringing more serenity and peace into your life. Learn more and more to free yourself from fears, anger, possessiveness, jealousy, etc., when they arise in your daily life. Freedom begins from the moment you become aware of the movements of your mind when they arise. Learn from facts, from what you are, simply theorizing will certainly not change you. You can learn many theories about anger, but only when it occurs in your life will it become a fact and, if you are able to manage anger becoming more and more aware of it, it will have less and less a grip on you, thus you will be more and more free. Learn to be comfortable with yourselves and do not make your happiness dependent on external factors. Love is freedom from all conditioning. Freedom is only in the here and now, and flourishes in the silence of the mind.

20. LIGHT

The idea of a fact is not the fact itself. The word light is not light. The idea that you have of light is not light itself, but it is only a description of it. All that can be described is not the truth. The light of awareness shows you what you really are in your daily life. Such a light burns thoughts in the bud. Offer your emotions and your dark feelings to the flame of awareness and everything will be reconciled. Be a light unto yourselves. Where there is light there can be no shadow. The I, seeking the Self, dissolves, like the moth that dies burned nearing the light of the flame. The light of awareness of what you are from moment to moment will bring more and more clarity and freedom into your lives and that of those who will come into contact with you.

21. LOVE

Never lose love and passion for the truth. The search for truth is the way of love. Love is truth, which is expressed through deeds in everyday life. Love is not doing to others what you would not want done to you. Love is committing yourself to being kinder to yourself and others. Love gives without asking anything in return, but love is also discernment. The knowledge of the Self opens the door to understanding and accepting diversity, which is love and compassion.

22. PURIFICATION OF BODY AND MIND

When you are in the dream or in the dreamless sleep state, you don't worry about purifying your body and mind. The problem arises in this state of consciousness, the waking state, which is not the only one. So, it depends from which perspective you look at. For example, if the observation of the problem occurs from the perspective of the Self, that is, from what you are before being born, or before the first birth, you will discover that who needs to be purified does not exist, therefore, the problem does not arise. If, on the other hand, the observation of the problem occurs from the perspective of the body-mind, then the thought of having to purify becomes, so to speak, real since it is supported not only by the idea of having to purify yourself from something, but also by identifying with your body and your mind. Both the body and the mind require a form of purification which, in this case, is understood as the ability to keep both healthy, through activities that allow the body to remain as healthy as possible and the mind to become more and more serene and silent. Let the mind relax and your heart will beat with love.

23. CHOICE

Where there is choice, there is confusion. Clarity requires no choices. In confusion, it is better not to choose, but rather take the time necessary until clarity dissolves all doubts, and then you will discover that there will be no need to choose, because you will know how to do the right thing, that is, what needs to be done. Remember that even not to choose is a choice. Your life will go on even if you happen to be unable to decide. But don't let others decide for your life. Total surrender to the divine will does not deny your capacity to choose but, on the contrary, frees you from selfishness so that you can decide for the common good.

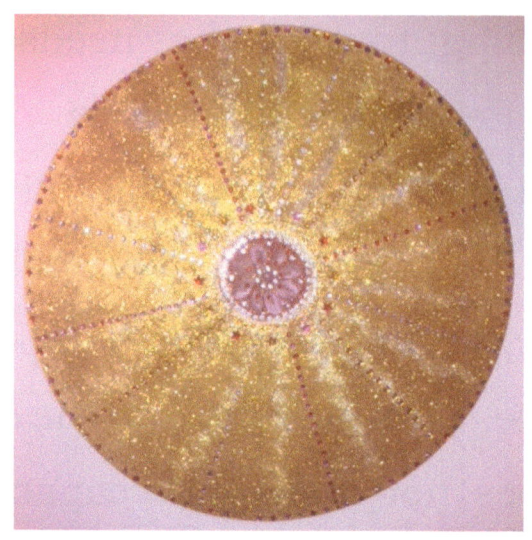

24. ETERNITY

You are eternal, but you continue not to believe it. In the physical plane it is impossible to realize eternity, you can only believe that it is so as long as you are in the body. The spiritual path is precisely this dis-identification from your body and mind, this will lead you back to eternity.

25. THE ACT OF OBSERVING

Thought creates the observer, the observed and the act of observing. Apparently, they seem separate, instead, they are one movement. You are what witnesses the arising and dissolution of your thoughts in your mind. You are the silence that is in your mind that precedes every thought. By becoming aware of the silence that reigns within you, your life will be more and more at peace, you will live more and more states of infinite bliss and ecstasy.

26. THE UNIVERSAL EVOLUTION

The qualities of your mind set the evaluation criteria. No one is better or worse than the other, you are all connected to each other and Love will make you understand that you are different but not separated from others. The paths are always different, but the source is the same for everyone.

27. SELF REALIZATION

In the different planes of consciousness there are different evolutionary degrees depending on the experiences lived by the soul. Anyone who manifests himself is subject to these laws. There is no evolution but only events that happen. Self-realization happens when you totally accept that you are the Absolute. When you realize the Self, the flame of pure awareness burns all that you are not, and what remains of you continues to exist, following its course, it is like turning off a fan switch, the propellers continue to turn until the energy has run out, just as your lives. No longer have any image of yourself, if it surfaces in your mind, burn it, sacrificing it, that is, making it sacred, on the flame of pure awareness, which has its roots in the peace of the mind. Only then will you truly be free from all conditioning.

You are the unchanging awareness that precedes both consciousness and unconsciousness.

28. THE SELF

The Self is the Absolute, therefore, it includes everything, knowledge and non-knowledge. There is nothing outside of the Self. Inner silence is the Self that unites and transcends everything and nothing; every separation dissolve.

29. THE ABSOLUTE, GOD

If it is not possible to accept that you are the Absolute, start by absolutely being convinced that you are the Absolute, dispelling any doubt from your mind. The sense of complete fulfilment in life is achieved by completely accepting what you are, the Absolute. Here every sense of separation dissolve.

CONCLUSION

We sincerely hope that these illuminating cards will help you bring freedom, light and love into your lives.

ISHVARA

FREEDOM * LIGHT * LOVE

Dawio Bordoli

Teacher of Shamanic Yoga, Imaginal Constellator, Musicoterapist, Reiki Master, Channelor, spiritual researcher, has created with his wife Therry different techniques of personal and spiritual growth such as Ishvara Amrita Yoga, Relational Constellations, Ishvara Healing

Meditation, Zen-Satsang and Creative Zen Painting; He leads groups for personal and spiritual growth and leads Kirtans / Bhajans. He has published 11 books.

Maria Theresia Bitterli

Master of Arts in Relational
Counseling, Bachelor of Science in
Communication, Constellator and
Imaginary Counselor,
Dramatherapist, Music Therapist,
Art Therapist, Reiki Master,

Naturopath, Channelor, Medium and Light Healer, AyurYoga and Yin Yoga teacher, Yesudian and Shamanic Yoga, Astrologer, spiritual researcher. Together with her husband Dawio, created various techniques of personal and spiritual growth such as Ishvara Amrita Yoga, Relational Constellations, Ishvara Healing Meditation, Zen-Satsang and Creative Zen Painting; she leads different groups of activities for personal and spiritual growth. She has published 18 books.

www.studioishvara.com